B

By Joanna Glum

Light in August
by William Faulkner

Bright
≡Summaries.com

WILLIAM FAULKNER

AMERICAN NOVELIST AND SCREENWRITER

- **Born in Mississippi, USA in 1897.**
- **Died in Mississippi, USA in 1962.**
- **Notable works:**
  - *The Sound and the Fury* (1929), novel
  - *As I Lay Dying* (1930), novel
  - *Absalom, Absalom!* (1936), novel

William Faulkner was an American novelist, screenwriter, and recipient of the Pulitzer Prize in Fiction (in 1955 and 1963) and the Nobel Prize in Literature (in 1949). Born and raised in Mississippi, Faulkner's early childhood was heavily influenced by his mother, his grandmother, and his African-American nanny, all of whom encouraged reading from a young age, as well as by his family's oral history of the Civil War and the old South. Though initially successful in school, Faulkner neither graduated from high school nor finished the courses he began at the University of Mississippi. Nonetheless, he was introduced to the work of James Joyce (Irish author, 1882-1941) and wrote poems as a young man, eventually publishing his first novel in 1929.

Though he suffered from alcoholism throughout his life, Faulkner had a prolific career, writing over 15 novels and the screenplays for such classic films as *To Have and Have Not* (1944) and *The Big Sleep* (1946). Noted for his modernist prose style, Faulkner's body of work made major contributions in the genre of the Southern Gothic, and his major works are regarded as some of the most influential and prominent novels of the 20th century.

LIGHT IN AUGUST

SOUTHERN GOTHIC NOVEL

- **Genre:** novel (modernist)
- **Reference edition:** Faulkner, W. (1993) *Light in August*. London: Picador.
- **1st edition:** 1932
- **Themes:** identity, prejudice (classist, racial, and religious), morality, gender politics, the burden of the past

Light in August focuses on the events surrounding the murder of a spinster in 1930s Mississippi; however, sprawling across an ensemble of characters and their remembered pasts, the novel depicts everything from religious extremism to misogyny to blatant racism. Culminating in the murder and castration of a man tormented throughout his life for having African-American blood, the novel observes a culture of conservatism and those who exist without it – from this racially-alienated man to an unwed pregnant woman to a delusional Reverend haunted by ghosts of the Civil War.

Light in August is an example of Faulkner at the height of his modernist techniques, and the novel has shifts not only in narrative time but also in point of view, with the same incidents being recounted and remembered by different characters in a way that revisits the immediate narrative past. The style recalls an oral tradition and, together with the thematic content, makes the novel a staple in the genre of the Southern Gothic.

SUMMARY

LENA ARRIVES IN JEFFERSON, WHERE A HOUSE IS ON FIRE

Lena Grove has left her brother's family in Alabama to seek Lucas Burch, the father of her illegitimate child who left town as soon as Lena became pregnant. Lena hitchhikes from town to town until she is finally picked up by Armstid, who brings her to his home on the way to Jefferson out of concern that she might deliver her baby soon. Though he introduces Lena to his wife as Lena Burch, Mrs. Armstid soon discerns that Lena is unmarried. Lena tries to convince Mrs. Armstid that Lucas is a good man despite his tendency to be jovial and to seek a good time.

Mrs. Armstid gives Lena the money she had saved from selling her eggs and sends her off. Armstid takes Lena to Varner's store, who informs Lena that the man at the Mill in Jefferson is named Bunch and not Burch. Nonetheless, she is taken to Jefferson and does not notice a house burning off the side of the road.

Byron Bunch recalls the day Joe Christmas arrived at the Mill and when Joe Brown arrived at the Mill. While Christmas arrived in new clothes the Monday following his first pay check, and continued to improve his condition over time, Brown did not. Bunch recalls that Brown would gamble away his money. He then recalls that Christmas quit first, followed by Brown, and that the two men had reputedly set up an illegal bootlegging business, all the while living in the former slave quarters on the property of an old, single woman and abolitionist named Burden. When Lena arrives at the Mill, Bunch immediately falls in love with her and regrets telling her that Joe Brown has a white scar above his mouth; this piece of information makes it clear that Joe Brown is Lucas Burch's pseudonym, and Lena is crestfallen.

Meanwhile, Reverend Gail Hightower observes the street from his study. He considers how Byron Bunch never goes to town with the other men on his night off, and how he discovered that Bunch instead goes to a church in another town during his time off. The narrator recounts the Reverend's life in Jefferson, where he no longer holds a parish and is an outcast, due largely to his wife's mental breakdown. Consumed with not only religion but also stories of his grandfather, a cavalryman killed in the Civil War, Hightower did not intervene with his wife's trips to Memphis, where she carried on an affair. Though she spent time in a sanatorium and ostensibly recovered, due to Hightower's neglect, she eventually relapsed and ultimately committed suicide. Hightower came under suspicion of carrying on an affair with his black cook, who then re-signed; however, the rumours effectively ruined Hightower's career, and he resigned after a few weeks of preaching to an empty parish.

Byron Bunch arrives at the Reverend's after having sent Lena to Mrs. Beard's boarding house, where Byron has been staying. He has convinced Mrs. Beard that Lena is in town to meet her husband and need only spend one night at the boarding house; Mrs. Beard allows it. Byron tells the Reverend that the Burden house is still on fire; he reveals that the previous day, when Lena arrived in town as the house began to burn, a man and his wife first entered the Burden house. The husband discovered Joe Brown distraught

downstairs, and when the man tried to go upstairs in order to retrieve the old woman, Brown
attempted to distract him. However, the man
made his way upstairs to discover the nearly
decapitated body of Joanna Burden, clearly the
victim of a violent attack. Joe Brown had gone by
the time the man returned downstairs.

Bunch continues to tell the Reverend that Joanna
Burden's nephew has offered a $1000 reward to
anyone who might apprehend the killer. Shortly
thereafter, Joe Brown informed the police that Joe
Christmas was the killer, revealing that Christmas
and Burden had been carrying on an affair since
Christmas arrived in Jefferson, as Brown noticed
that Christmas would leave their shared cabin
in the evenings to visit the main house. Brown
continued that Christmas threatened to kill him if
he were to reveal any information about the affair
with Burden. He says that Christmas told him
that he had killed Joanna Burden on the day of the
fire, and while the police did not initially believe
Brown's story, after he said that Christmas is in
fact part black, the sheriff immediately believed it.
Nonetheless, the police kept Brown apprehended
as they opened up a search for Christmas. Byron

tells the Reverend that he has not told Lena of this news, saying that he had worried that Brown might attempt to leave town once more.

The narrator returns to the days prior to the fire, detailing how Joe Brown arrived that evening drunk and loud. Joe Christmas had been unable to sleep, and, further riled by Brown's behaviour, throws him down and beat him. Though Brown calls Christmas a "nigger" (p.79) seemingly in an attempt to hurt him, Brown finally passes out from drink and sleep. Christmas lies awake in his bed thinking "God loves me too" (p. 80). He considers how Joanna Burden not only lied to him about his age but had also prayed over him after he had left her bed. While he says he might be able to forgive the former, he cannot forgive the latter. He gets out of bed, strips, and heads to the road, where he screams at a woman passing by in a car. He finally sleeps for a few hours in the stables on Burden's property.

In the morning, Christmas goes to a clearing on the property; he shaves, reads a magazine, and pours out the whisky hidden in a tin. He puts the empty tins back. Christmas thinks about how he loathes Brown as he watches him receive a shave at a barbershop that night. Christmas then goes to the part of the town where the black residents live, before moving to the white part of town. He continues to walk and, while on the road, "he could smell negro" (p. 90). He nearly assaults a group of black man with a razor he had not realised he was holding. He snaps out of it, and then heads back to the Burden house, thinking "something is going to happen to me" (p. 91).

JOE CHRISTMAS' LIFE

The narrator turns to Joe Christmas' earlier life, when he had lived in an orphanage. As a five-year-old, he would eat the toothpaste of a woman in the orphanage who monitored the children's diets. He does this every night, until one night he is nearly caught when the woman returns to her room with a man. Though Joe hides behind a curtain, he begins to hear them having sex and, having eaten toothpaste, he vomits. The woman throws him out of the room, calling him a "little nigger bastard" (p. 94).

The woman then believes that Joe will cost her her job by telling the orphanage director that she is carrying on an affair. Though she attempts to offer him money to keep quiet, Joe does not understand the consequences of what he saw. He refuses the money. The woman then approaches the janitor, who reveals that Joe is biracial. While she asks the janitor to offer this information to the orphanage matron, the janitor refuses, knowing that Joe would then have to be transferred to a black orphanage.

The janitor remains preoccupied about the boy and confronts the woman, who informs him that she intends to tell the matron that Joe is half black. The janitor then takes matters into his own hands and takes Joe away, "enveloped in the man's coat" (p. 106). However, he and Joe are arrested in Little Rock, and Joe is sent back to the orphanage. The woman quickly makes sure that Joe is adopted by a farmer named Mr. McEachern, whose sober religiosity makes him condemn Joe's surname of Christmas, which Joe had been given after having been found on Christmas Eve on the steps of the orphanage. McEachern renames Joe with his own surname.

Having lived with McEachern for three years, Joe has yet to learn the catechism by heart. McEachern tells Joe that he may have one hour to try to learn again, but Joe fails to learn the catechism, and McEachern takes him to the stable and whips him. Joe is "calm, peaceful, quite inscrutable" (p. 116) as McEachern beats him unconscious. When he wakes up, he is in his own bed with McEachern next to him, who asks Joe to pray for forgiveness. He gives Joe the catechism once more and leaves for church. McEachern's wife brings Joe food despite the fact that McEachern had requested that he not be served any. Joe refuses the food and throws it to the floor. Mrs. McEachern leaves, and later that night, Joe gives in to his hunger and eats the food off of the floor, "like a dog" (p. 118).

When Joe is a teenager, he and other boys from the farm trick a young black woman into one of their sheds. She appears willing to have sex, and each boy takes his turn with her. However, when it comes time for Joe to have sex with her, he instead beats her up, until "there was no She at all now" (p. 119). The others eventually pull him off her with difficulty. Joe is eventually released and goes home to be punished by his father for not having finished his work on the farm that evening. McEachern asks Joe if he has been with a woman and asks if he left marks on the boys he was fighting.

A few years later, Joe buys a suit for himself by selling McEachern's calf. McEachern finds it tucked into the hay loft and the calf missing, but when he confronts Joe, Joe unintentionally lies and says "with a kind of shocked astonishment" (p. 125) that Mrs. McEachern took the cow for Joe. McEachern continues his inquisition, and he eventually accuses Joe of "lying and lechery" (*ibid.*). He punches Joe in the face, but Joe tells McEachern to stop given that Joe could easily cause serious damage to the old man. That night, Mrs. McEachern tries to convince her husband that she herself purchased the suit for Joe with her own money from selling butter, but McEachern does not believe her and forces her to pray, seeking forgiveness from God.

Joe thinks that Mrs. McEachern has throughout his life tried to be like a mother to him, particularly in trying to save Joe from her husband's abuse, but Joe considers how her kindness made him unable to endure McEachern's abuse because she, in her care, ultimately made the beatings seem personal. Joe concludes that he hates Mrs. McEachern more in her kindness than her husband in his abuse. He thinks that "she is trying to make [him] cry" (p. 128).

That night while the McEacherns sleep, Joe sneaks out of his room by descending a rope he had tied from his bedroom window. He heads to the barn, retrieves his suit and a new watch, and waits on the road for a date to pick him up to go dancing. Joe had met the woman while on a trip into town with McEachern, who had gone to town to meet his lawyer. After his meeting, which ran late, McEachern took Joe to a run-down restaurant that he forbids Joe from entering again, calling it a place "where a man may go but a boy...may not" (p. 132). However, the next time Joe goes into town with McEachern on a trip to the lawyer, he visits the restaurant with a dime that McEachern had given him. Joe orders from the same waitress he had met on his first trip to the restaurant, and when he comes up short to pay for all of his food, the waitress pays for the rest of it.

Upset by how attracted he is to the woman, Joe tries to avoid going to town by throwing himself into his work, for which McEachern rewards him with a new cow. However, on McEachern's next trip into town, Joe goes with him and heads to the restaurant. He tries to pay the restaurant back for his previous meal with some money that Mrs. McEachern had given him. However, the waitress is not there and the men laugh at Joe for trying to repay her. He runs into the street only to run into the waitress, Bobbie Allen, and the two arrange to meet a few nights later. He tells her that his surname is Christmas, not McEachern.

Joe arrives early and thinks that she will not arrive, thinking "in a moment she will vanish" (p. 142). When Bobbie arrives, she tells Joe that she is sick, and given that he has never been with a woman nor been taught about women, Joe fails to realise that she is on her period. He hits her and leaves. However, the two meet again the following week, and Joe takes her rather forcibly into nearby foliage and loses his virginity to her. They begin to meet regularly, with Joe paying Bobbie with money he has stolen from Mrs. McEachern. Joe does not understand the repercussions of his payments, unaware that Bobbie is really a prostitute who works for the couple who own the restaurant. Joe later takes his first drink with Bobbie on a visit to the restaurant's owners with her.

On one of his nights with Bobbie, Joe confesses that he suspects that he is "more than just a foreigner" (p. 148), and indeed that he has African-American heritage. One night, Bobbie does not appear for her date with Joe. Angry, he goes to her house and sees her in the window with another man. When Joe meets up with her on their next date, he beats her until he exhausts himself. She then finally tells him that she is a prostitute. This calms Joe down, and he proceeds to steal money from Mrs. McEachern, who notices the pattern of behaviour while Mr. McEachern remains totally unaware. However, McEachern eventually catches on, seeing that the hidden suit has been worn.

McEachern catches Joe sneaking out of his window one night, and he follows him into town. He barges into the local schoolhouse, which is hosting a dance, and he immediately begins to beat Joe while hurling slurs at Bobbie, calling her "Jezebel" (p. 154). In retaliation, Joe grabs a chair and hits McEachern over the head, killing him. Joe immediately steals McEachern's horse and rides to their home, where he takes the money that Mrs. McEachern had been saving from under a floorboard. Joe leaves his house, eventually running to the restaurant owners' house, where Bobbie packs her bags, ready to leave town. She condemns Joe for having pulled her into trouble, which could threaten the state of the restaurant and brothel. Joe, "in a quiet, dreamlike state" (p. 163), tries to propose to her, offering her the money he stole from his house. She refuses, hurling a racial slur at Joe, which in turn causes the group of men in the room to beat Joe into a near comatose state. One of the restaurant owners stops them from doing further damage. Joe listens as the group decides to take the money Joe had meant to give the waitress, and they leave. One of the owners puts her own money in Joe's trouser pocket, and when Joe wakes from his beaten state, he staggers outside and leaves town.

Joe begins an itinerant life, hitchhiking from town to town and working odd jobs on farms, mines, and oil fields. At one point, he joins the army but eventually deserts, living for a time in black communities, "shunning white people" (p. 170). Joe continues to seek the company of prostitutes, revealing to them that he has 'Negro' blood, which in turns causes all of the prostitutes to reject him without seeking payment. However, at one point, Joe encounters a prostitute who does not care whether or not he is black, and this in turn causes Joe to beat her senseless. Afterwards, he gets ill. Joe spends time in a predominantly black town and takes up with a black woman before eventually arriving in Jefferson, where he enquires about the Burden plantation. He sneaks into Joanna Burden's kitchen that night and eats leftover food on the counter. Joanna Burden enters, and while Joe does not flee, she does not tell him to leave. Instead, she lets him finish eating, and the two begin their relationship.

Their affair is loveless, and Joe remains in the kitchen during the day, where he sneaks in to eat the food set out "for the nigger" (p. 179) by Burden. At night, Joe goes to her bedroom, where the two have sex, Joe feeling the need to dominate her. At one point, Burden makes a full meal for Joe, but, upon discovering it, he throws the dishes and food against the wall. Joe eventually obtains a job at the lumber mill and ceases to see Burden despite living in the cabin on her property. One night in September, he returns to his cabin to find Burden waiting for him, and she begins to tell him her family story, including that of her grandfather and brother, who were killed over a disagreement with a local white man about black voting rights. Joe reveals to her that one of his parents was black.

Joe and Joanna Burden meet only at night, and Joe watches Burden "pass through every avatar of a woman in love" (p. 194). They begin to play a game of hide-and-seek as a form of foreplay and have sex outside on the property. However, their relationship eventually grows stale as Burden begins "to get fat" (p. 196). Joe begins to sell liquor from the property and goes to Memphis to sell and to sleep with prostitutes. At one point, Burden asks Joe for a child, and while he says "No at once" (p. 199), she reveals just after Christmastime that she is pregnant. By the time the winter comes, the two have stopped sleeping together, but one night, Joe comes home to find a note from Burden asking to see him. He goes to the house, where Burden tells Joe he ought not to waste his life and should take over her position as advisor at the black colleges around town, which Joe rebukes, thinking that "it was because she was pregnant" (p. 202) that she is saying such things. He is perturbed by her and her comments.

Joe Brown comes to stay in the cabin with Christmas. At one point, Brown mocks Christmas for "tomcat[ting] to" (p. 206) Burden, and Joe beats him until he goes away. Burden leaves Christmas another note, and he goes upstairs to her bedroom to find her waiting for him. She says that she will cover the fees to send Joe to a black college to learn law, at which point he might able to train with a black lawyer in Memphis and take over Burden's business. Joe is enraged, hits Burden, and leaves. Regardless, Burden continues to summon Joe, and one night, he goes to her room carrying a razor. He finds Burden praying, and she asks Joe to kneel and pray with her. However, he refuses, and Burden reveals that she is holding a revolver, which she fires.

Joe finds himself suddenly trying to get the attention of a car driving down the road. Frightened, the man driving leaves Joe behind. Joe walks down the road and ultimately discovers that he is holding Burden's revolver, which is unfired and contains two bullets. This leads Joe to surmise that not only did Burden fail to shoot, but that she had intended to take her own life after taking Joe's.

INVESTIGATING THE MURDER OF JOANNA BURDEN

Returning to the action from the beginning of the novel with Burden's house ablaze, people begin to gather around the fire. The sheriff removes Burden's body from the house as Jefferson's new fire truck arrives but is left unable to put out the fire given that there is no source of water into which to tap. The sheriff notices that the cabin appears to have been occupied. He begins to question a neighbourhood black man about the cabin and its occupants, believing he will find the killer in the black part of town. Unable to get the response he wants, the sheriff resorts to whipping the man with a belt until the man says that he "heard talk about how two white men" (p. 220) had been living in the cabin. From another man, the sheriff discovers that the two men are Joe Christmas and Joe Brown. He leaves the plantation and goes back to town followed by a caravan of travellers. They stop as Lena Grove is let off her wagon.

The sheriff retrieves a letter that Joanna Burden had left at the bank and opens it. It is inscribed from her lawyer, to whom they refer as "a nigger lawyer" (p. 221), and the sheriff sends messages to both Burden's lawyer in Memphis and her nephew in New Hampshire. The latter responds that he will pay a reward of $1000 to anyone who can identify the killer, prompting Joe Brown to immediately arrive at the police station claiming that Joe Christmas is the killer, and they take him to the jail "for safekeeping" (p. 222). A man who drove Christmas to the station confirms Brown's story, and the sheriff subsequently sends out a search party, but they are unable to find Christmas.

All the while, Bunch and the Reverend talk about Lena, with Bunch saying that he would like Lena to be moved out of the boarding house in which he had set her up. However, the Reverend suggests that in her pregnant state, she might best be taken care of at the boarding house, "with a woman at hand if she should need one" (p. 225). Bunch again is frustrated by having inadvertently told Lena about Joe Brown being Lucas Burch, but he convinces himself it is best she knows that Burch is "a scoundrel" (p. 228).

Lena later asks Bunch to go to where Brown/Burch had been staying and wait until he returns. Bunch assumes that if he tells Brown/Burch that

Lena is waiting for him in Jefferson, Brown/Burch will leave town, leaving Lena somewhat available for the lovelorn Bunch. However, he also considers that Brown/Burch might marry Lena with the money he would receive from the reward for having identified Burden's killer. Hightower considers how he has heard reports that the search party is close to finding Christmas as Bunch arrives. He tells the Reverend that he has moved Lena into the old cabin on the Burden property but that he is living in a tent on the property to ensure her safety. The Reverend tells Bunch that no woman deserves more than either a Lucas Burch or a Byron Bunch, ostensibly counselling Bunch away from caring for Lena, but he ultimately says that he will support Bunch when the time comes, thinking "to be young. There is nothing else like it" (p. 239).

Meanwhile, a deputy tells the sheriff that Lena has moved into the cabin because she thinks it is "the one that Lucas Burch had promised to get ready for her to live in" (p. 241). The sheriff chooses not to pursue Lena or Bunch, whom he knows is living nearby on the property, saying that they are not going to cause any trouble.

Early that morning, a man calls the sheriff to him in order to report a rampage at a black church in another town. The man says that someone he identifies as Joe Christmas stormed into the church, attacking multiple people in the parish, and taking to the pulpit until a woman proclaimed "it's Satan himself" (p. 242). The grandson of one of Joe's victims tried to subdue Joe with a razor, but Joe overpowered him and knocked him out. Joe eventually ran off.

The sheriff sends the search party with bloodhounds to the church, but all they find is a note to the sheriff. The party moves onward, eventually discovering a cabin where they discover only that Christmas has left his shoes and traded with the woman inside. The sheriff redirects the search, but they find nothing. Meanwhile, Christmas collapses. He has eaten nothing and has slept intermittently. Exhausted, he finds decomposing fruit and picks premature corn from a nearby field, both of which he eats. Whenever he encounters people, they "halt, dead, looking at him with whiterolling eyes" (p. 253). In a delirium, he barely recalls being fed a full meal by a black family before being able to catch a ride into Mottstown.

In Mottstown, the impoverished and crazed Mr. Hines and his wife have settled after he lost his job in Memphis, and they appear to subsist merely on the charity of a few black women who have brought them food for the past 25 years. Mr. Hines has become a de facto preacher at a local black church, where he barges unwanted into the service to preach white superiority, telling the parishioners to have "humility before all skins lighter than theirs" (p. 258). Mr. Hines encounters Joe Christmas when he is brought into town, having been captured by the man who had offered him a ride. Mr. Hines tries to assault Christmas when he sees him, but he is brought home, where his wife asks Mr. Hines what he did with "Milly's baby" (p. 262). The people of the town speculate about Christmas, saying that he does not look black. An unnamed group discuss the details of what occurred. As they are talking, Mr. Hines arrives back in town asking that Christmas be killed rather than returned to Jefferson, and he riles up a crowd. Meanwhile, Mrs. Hines tries to find the sheriff so that she may be granted permission to see Joe. However, a group from Jefferson arrives to return Christmas to their jurisdiction for his trial, but the crowd

that has formed teem around the prison deman-
ding that Christmas be put to death. Christmas is
led safely to the cars just as Mrs. Hines is able to
make her way to him. She does nothing but look
at him, and then she leaves, and the crowd stays
still for a moment. Mrs. Hines tries to hire a car to
drive to Jefferson, but they are all too expensive,
and she eventually buys two train tickets and
waits at the station with Mr. Hines, who screams
"bitchery and abomination" (p. 272) as they wait
for their early morning train.

Meanwhile, Bunch arrives at the Reverend's to
tell him that Christmas has been captured. The
Reverend accuses Bunch of being sinful and of
taking advantage of the situation in order to
quench his own desires for Lena. Hightower
thinks about how he feels "dissociated from
mechanical time" (p. 275), how he passes
through life observing pain and pleasure in
those around him, be they good or bad, and
how all ultimately descend into "drinking and
fighting and praying" (p. 276). He sees Bunch return to his home with Mr. and Mrs. Hines. Bunch
reveals that Christmas is "their daughter's
child" (p. 278), whom Mr. Hines had taken away

after his daughter, Milly, had given birth. Mr. Hines interrupts the conversation throughout, lamenting his daughter's deprivation and calling for Christmas to be lynched. Mrs. Hines tells Bunch and the Reverend that her daughter Milly had been having an affair with a man who had worked in a passing circus who claimed to be Mexican, though he was in fact part black. Mr. Hines stopped his daughter from running away with him by killing him. Though he initially attempted to find a doctor to abort Milly's baby, he eventually was unable to due to his religious beliefs. He instead violently assaulted a doctor before brandishing a gun in a church, claiming that the devil had won. He was arrested, and when he was released, he found that Milly had gone into labour at his house. Though Mrs. Hines asked that he retrieve a doctor, he refused and beat his wife. Milly eventually died in labour. Mrs. Hines discovered one day that the baby had gone.

Meanwhile, Mr. Hines left Joe at an orphanage on Christmas Eve and arranged to work there while Joe was there. He used to watch Joe and saw him stop playing with the kids as their racial slurs grew worse and more frequent, though Hines also addressed Joe with racial slurs. After Joe found the dietician having sex, Hines discovered that Joe had been adopted out, so he told his wife that Joe had died.

Hightower tries to determine the point of the Hines' story and why Bunch had brought them to meet him. Mrs. Hines says that she wants Christmas out for just one day, "like the world never had anything against him yet" (p. 292), and Byron asks that the Reverend produce a false alibi for Christmas by saying that Christmas was with him on the night of the murder. The Reverend balks at this and turns them out.

The next morning, Lena has her baby. Bunch seeks the Reverend's help in the delivery of the baby before hurriedly running off to obtain a doctor. The doctor he finds is the same one who had arrived late to the delivery of the black baby which Hightower had overseen, and he is also slow to ready himself this time, ultimately unable to find his keys. Bunch and the doctor head to the cabin, where they discover that Lena has already given birth. Hightower and Mr. and Mrs. Hines are there, the former asleep on the cot and the latter in a state of delusion, referring to Lena as Milly and the baby as Joe as she holds it. It occurs to Bunch that he had forgotten to arrange a doctor initially because he did not believe that the baby would come. He takes off to find Joe Brown/Lucas Burch to tell him that Lena has had his baby.

The Reverend returns home, where he falls asleep in his yard. When he wakes up, he returns to the cabin to find Lena alone. She says that Mr. Hines had left without his wife, but that Mrs. Hines followed shortly after once she had awoken. Lena confesses that she was troubled by Mrs. Hines' claim that her baby was the child of Joe Christmas. She tells the Reverend that Bunch had gone to town to release Brown/Burch from jail so that he might visit her and the baby, so the Reverend heads into town. He discovers that Bunch has quit his job at the Mill and heads to the courthouse to find him.

There, the grand jury convenes. Bunch is uncomfortable being Lena's advocate, given that she is "another man's whore" (p. 313), and thinks about how he would not have had the opportunity to be hurt had he not begun to care about someone else. He finds that his possessions have been packed away at the boarding house. Eventually, Bunch meets with the sheriff, who agrees to let Brown go to visit Lena, where Bunch hides himself nearby to watch an officer force Brown/Burch into the cabin. Bunch packs his mule and takes off, but he stops when he sees Brown/Burch running away from the cabin. Bunch pursues him on his mule.

The narrative shifts to Brown/Burch as he is pulled from jail, unaware of where he is going. He is brought to Lena and grows infuriated, and the two size each other up, with Lena thinking she knows how Brown/Burch will try to lie as though the cabin were the one he had promised her. He does lie to her, saying that he sent money to Lena but that it must not have reached her because the messenger was not trustworthy. He eventually runs away from the cabin and happens upon another cabin belonging to a black family, where he finds a boy whom he pays to send a message to the sheriff for the receipt of the reward money. The messenger encounters Bunch on the road and points him in Brown/Burch's direction.

Bunch confronts him, pulling him into a physical brawl, but Brown/Burch overpowers Bunch and leaves him bleeding on the ground. Bunch comes to and walks to the railroad, where he can just make out Brown/Burch jumping onto a train, "passing one another as though on opposite orbits and with an effect as of phantoms or apparitions" (p. 332). Bunch, still thrown by the fight, tries to make his way back to Lena, but he is stopped by a passer-by who tells him that Christmas has been killed.

Mr. and Mrs. Hines are assured by the district attorney that Christmas' body will be sent to them the following day. They board a train back to Mottstown. One of the district attorney's former school friends from his days at Harvard arrives as Mr. and Mrs. Hines leave, and he and Stevens discuss how Christmas was discovered in the Reverend's home after having escaped. Though the Reverend had a pistol, he was scared away from action, and watched as a group of white supremacists shot Christmas to death.

The narrative then recounts the life of Percy Grimm, a white supremacist who further be-lieves that "the American is superior to all other white races" (p. 339). Though not a part of the American Legion, a fault he blames on his parents, Grimm had already come to command a small contingency of its members. He follows Christmas' case closely, ordering a small patrol to keep watch before the Grand Jury, and when Christmas escapes in Jefferson, Grimm takes off in pursuit of him. Three others join him and discover Christmas in the Reverend's house, where, with "shameless savageness" (p. 348), they kill Christmas despite the Reverend's protests and assertions that Christmas had been there with him on the night of Joanna Burden's murder. Grimm shoots Christmas multiple times and, before Christmas dies, finally castrates him with a butcher knife from the Reverend's kitchen.

Later, the Reverend considers how he never revealed his true thoughts on his past to even his wife when they were in love, and he chronicles how his grandfather had owned slaves and had never understood how Hightower's father could choose to be both an abolitionist and a preacher. The Reverend's father was a pacifist and never fired his weapon when he was made to serve for the South in the Civil War, and his grandfather was killed during the war. He thinks on his own life, having sought belonging and meaning in the seminary and then in Jefferson. He finally thinks of "all the faces which he has even seen" (p. 369), including those of Lena, Bunch, and Christmas, and thinks about time dissolving until his thoughts rest on the sounds of bugle and cavalry officers.

In the final chapter, a furniture repairman and dealer recounts how on his way back through to Tennessee he picked up a man and woman whom he suspected to be man and wife. They are in fact Lena and Byron Bunch, whom he discovers to be unmarried when they stop for the night to camp out. That night, Lena sleeps in the back of the man's truck while Bunch moves off elsewhere, having been denied the ability to sleep in the truck by Lena. She assumes that he will not return the next morning, but the man recalls how, driving down the road with Lena, they picked up Bunch once again. He and Lena travel on, searching for Lucas Burch, with Lena thinking about how far she has travelled, as she had thought at the beginning of the novel when she arrived in Jackson.

CHARACTER STUDY

LENA GROVE

Lena Grove both brings the reader into the events of the novel and carries them out, providing a narrative throughline in the novel; in fact, the birth of her baby occurs simultaneously with the other dramatic climaxes within the novel. Orphaned at 12, Lena lived with her much older brother before becoming pregnant with Lucas Burch's baby. Seemingly complacent about her lot in life, Lena makes her way from town to town through the generosity of others while never wanting to feel obliged to them; furthermore, she continues to seek Burch despite ostensibly knowing that he will never settle down with her. She is introduced as walking barefoot so that "people who saw her and whom she passed on foot would believe that she lived in the town too" (p. 5); in this way, her character can be interpreted as one seeking belonging and her departure from town at the close of the novel suggests, perhaps, that she may never be rooted.

JOE CHRISTMAS

One of the three major figures in the novel, Joe
Christmas was left at an orphanage as a child by
grandparents who condemned him. Being part
African-American yet appearing white, Joe is
consistently ostracised from every environment
in which he finds himself, and he develops violent
behaviours at a young age. In particular, Joe
exhibits violent tendencies towards women and
towards people who treat him kindly. His vio-
lence against others and his homicidal tendencies can be interpreted as a means of dissociating
others from their humanity and their identities
in the same way that he is made to dissociate
from himself. His self-destructive nature can be
seen as his way of wrestling with his identity that
has ostensibly condemned him from birth, not
knowing when he was young that "his own flesh
as well as all space was still a cage" (p. 122).

REVEREND GAIL HIGHTOWER

Reverend Hightower completes the major trio of
characters in the novel. A neurotic figure, he is
haunted by the memories not only of his ill-fated

wife, whose perceived moral depravity lost the Reverend his parish, but also of the ghost of his grandfather, who was a cavalryman in the Civil War. Hightower's perspective provides a kind of detached objectivity on the action, and he ultimately bears witness to both Lena's labour and to Christmas' murder. He ultimately replays the events of the novel, as well as of his remembered family history, in an attempt to exorcise the past, "so that it can be Now" (p. 370).

LUCAS BURCH/JOE BROWN

Identified by the "small white scar beside the mouth" (p. 29), Lucas Burch is the father of Lena Grove's baby. When he discovers her pregnancy, he leaves her and escapes to Jefferson, where he finds work under the false name of Joe Brown. When confronted with Lena and their baby in the novel's finale, Burch runs away once again, suggesting that his penchant for a careless and carefree existence will continue. Utterly irresponsible, he makes a clumsy business partner for Joe Christmas, whom he ultimately turns in in order to collect reward money.

BYRON BUNCH

Though he had always preferred to spend his time alone, given his withdrawn and quiet nature, Byron Bunch immediately falls in love with Lena Grove when he first sees her. He spends much of the novel attempting to help her with her pregnancy, confiding in the Reverend his feelings for her and the conflict he feels about disclosing Burch's identity to Lena. He ultimately quits his job and joins Lena on the road to find Burch once more, proving to be the only consistent figure in Lena's life. Though more reserved than either Brown or Christmas, Bunch nonetheless displays a casually misogynistic view of women.

JOANNA BURDEN

Joanna, like the Reverend Hightower, is an outsider in the town of Jefferson. Given that her family supported the rights of African-Americans and maintained ties with both the black community and abolitionists, she is left as isolated on her property as Hightower is on his. Her relationship with Christmas is passionate, but at times her desire for him to improve himself and reach his potential is conflated with a kind of missionary religiosity. Ultimately, she succumbs to an obsessive and passionate love for him.

ANALYSIS

OUTSIDERS AND THEIR IDENTITIES

Littering his text with boarding houses and orphanages, whorehouses and derelict cabins, Faulkner's landscape is a landscape built to both breed and sustain outcasts from the broader society of the American South. Structuring the narrative around journeys from town to town, Faulkner creates a network of outsiders ostensibly on personal journeys to find belonging. Particularly with the character of Christmas, Faulkner observes the ways in which a fractured identity in the Southern interwar landscape is unable to find any root, saying that Christmas "thought that is was loneliness which he was trying to escape and not himself" (p. 170). Indeed, with Lena Grove's quest to find her baby's father despite Burch's clear unwillingness to settle down. Faulkner seems to represent people on the fringes of society looking for purpose and place in one another; the quest to solve a basic loneliness is married to the broader existential struggle to derive or construct authentic identity. The confidence between Hightower and Bunch, the relationship between Burden and Christmas, and Lena's journey between the homes of strangers suggests a texture of figures who seek similarly alienated members of an otherwise normative society in order to survive.

NORMATIVITY: RELIGION, GENDER POLITICS, AND RACIAL PREJUDICE

Faulkner's outsiders are made so by virtue of the overwhelmingly bigoted and conservative nature of their society, represented in microcosm by the town of Jefferson. The predominant social models are those of religion, gender politics, and racial prejudice, and every character, even those persecuted by others, exhibit in some way aspects of these influences.

Much has been made of the religious overtones of Faulkner's text, observing that Joe Christmas is persecuted and killed at the age of 33, the age at which Christ was put to death. Indeed, the motif of trinities is predominant throughout, with Joe Christmas remembering moments in his life as sequences of three, and Faulkner does create a trinity of three main characters in his text. However, while these interpretations are not without merit, they perhaps are not as relevant as Faulkner's conflation of religion with other forms of prejudice. Hightower, most significantly, cannot practice his faith when his parish condemns his personal life as sinful, creating an ironic juxtaposition of religious faith against the social conservatism and exclusion it engenders.

Hightower, Hines, and McEachern, for example, all exhibit misogynistic tendencies, the latter two using the Biblical name Jezebel against women. Even Hightower, who is markedly less violent and prejudiced than the other two men, exhibits condescending views toward women, and throughout the novel, advocates are proven to regurgitate the same kind of prejudices as open enemies. For example, Lena's first advocate on her journey, Armstid, observes that "womenfolks are likely to be good without being very kind" (p. 12), and indeed Lena meets the generosity of strangers throughout her journey while never gaining social acceptance as a result of her condition, condemned by the socially and religiously conservative community.

Similarly, while Joanna Burden is ostensibly on a mission to help Joe, particularly when she discovers that he is mixed race and therefore made a pariah by every community in which he has ever lived, she ultimately attempts to take his life for not fulfilling the life she had envisioned for him. Indeed, Christmas is the most tragic symbol of the effects of normative prejudice. With non-normative relationships with women, a lack of religious practice, and being neither black nor white, Christmas engages in a self-destruction that can be seen as an attempt to escape his particular social prison.

Faulkner is able to observe these prejudices of the American South by moving between different voices. Most significantly, he is able to ventriloquise the ubiquitous and casual racism proven to ultimately damn Christmas by detailing the conversation of unnamed locals, who gossip about the events of Christmas' arrest and use frequently the word 'nigger.' Indeed, this slur proliferates throughout the text, and by showing the consequences of the racism that breeds this language, Faulkner seems to suggest that culture is informed by the language and stories of others.

GHOSTS OF THE PAST AND THE AMERICAN SOUTH

Faulkner choses to frame his story in his contemporary interwar period of the American South, an environment ravaged not only by the Civil War but also by the Reconstruction period that followed. His text is written in a way that evokes a sense of oral tradition, blending narrative modes and creating a polyphony of voices, asserting that the events of the story are only manifested through the collective telling and retelling by an entire community. In effect, Faulkner confirms the reality-making nature of storytelling in this way and further conflates history with fiction, asserting that power remains in the hands of those who are able to articulate their stories.

Time is fluid and fractured throughout the novel, blending the events of the 'present' with not only 'present' recollections of past events but with narrative scenes of the past themselves. In this way, the dialogue itself is haunted. By putting remembered dialogue in italics as opposed to quotation marks, Faulkner creates the imprint of something said without quoting it directly, as though what remains is the impression made to someone but not necessarily the words themselves.

Through the Reverend, Faulkner seems to suggest a generation haunted by the ghosts of the Civil War and its racist implications. The stasis in which the Reverend finds himself can be more broadly applied to the landscape of Jefferson itself, caught in the stasis of a seemingly endless summer. When Christmas dies, he appears to "rise soaring into their memories forever and ever" (p. 349), further suggesting that the implications of a land built upon absolutism and persecution will live on.

FURTHER REFLECTION

SOME QUESTIONS TO THINK ABOUT...

- Discuss the nature of time throughout the novel. What does Faulkner seem to suggest by not only replaying events but by having characters consider the ways in which they process time personally?
- What do the final lines of the novel suggest with regards to Lena Grove's journey? Will she ever abandon her quest to find Lucas Burch?
- Why is this novel considered a work of Southern Gothic fiction? Are the ghosts that haunt the Reverend to be interpreted literally or metaphorically? Explain your answer.
- What does Joe Christmas' eating of toothpaste as a boy have to do with his overall character? What might be said about his conflict with compulsion?
- What does Faulkner achieve by recounting Joe Christmas' past? Why does he not merely choose to recount the events of the 'present'?

- Are any characters 'good'? If so, whom? Are any characters 'bad'? If so, whom? In either case, how does Faulkner either judge or choose to withhold moral judgment?

We want to hear from you!
Leave a comment on your online library
and share your favourite books on social media!

FURTHER READING

REFERENCE EDITION

- Faulkner, W. (1993) *Light in August*. London: Picador.

REFERENCE STUDIES

- Anderson, J. (2007) *Student Companion to William Faulkner*. Westport: Greenwood Press.

- Hamblin, R., ed (1999) *A William Faulkner Encyclopedia*. Westport: Greenwood Press.

- Hamblin, R. (2016) *Myself and the World: A Biography of William Faulkner*. Jackson: University Press of Mississippi.

- Matthews, J., ed. (2015) *The New Cambridge Companion to William Faulkner*. Cambridge: Cambridge University Press.

- Ruppersburg, H. (1994) *Reading Faulkner: Light in August*. Jackson: University Press of Mississippi.

- Williamson, J. (1995) *William Faulkner and Southern History*. Oxford: Oxford University Press.

ADDITIONAL SOURCES

- Milgate, M. (1987) *New Essays on Light in August*. Cambridge: Cambridge University Press.

- Parini, J. (2009) *One Matchless Time: A Life of William Faulkner*. New York: HarperCollins.

MORE FROM BRIGHTSUMMARIES.COM

- Reading guide – *As I Lay Dying* by William Faulkner.

- Reading guide – *Sanctuary* by William Faulkner.

- Reading guide – *The Sound and the Fury* by William Faulkner.

- Reading guide – *The Wishing Tree* by William Faulkner.